F. W Conquest

**First Steps in Latin Grammar**

F. W Conquest

**First Steps in Latin Grammar**

ISBN/EAN: 9783337302924

Printed in Europe, USA, Canada, Australia, Japan

Cover: Foto ©Paul-Georg Meister /pixelio.de

More available books at **www.hansebooks.com**

# First Steps

in

# Latin Grammar.

by

## F. W. CONQUEST, B.A.

---

## THIRD EDITION

---

LONDON:
PUBLISHED BY RELFE, BROTHERS,
6, CHARTERHOUSE BUILDINGS, ALDERSGATE.

# PREFACE.

*Many teachers who have had to take a class of young beginners in Latin, have doubtless found it difficult to keep the little ones employed. A declension is soon learnt, but as soon forgotten. Time and exercise are needed to fix it thoroughly in the mind. This little book is put forth in the hope of diminishing this difficulty. It is intended for boys and girls beginning their Latin at about nine or ten years of age, and is believed to contain a very fair half-year's work for such.*

*If when seated at the desk every other child does a B exercise, it will do away with a great deal of copying.*

# FIRST STEPS IN LATIN GRAMMAR.

WE begin to-day to learn *Latin*, a language once spoken by the greatest people in the world, namely the Romans

Rome was the chief city of Latium, a country on the western coast of Italy, and the people living in Latium were called Latins. The Romans then spoke Latin ; and we all know that they conquered a large part of the world and in this way they carried their language not only over all Italy, but also over Spain, Portugal, France, Switzerland, and Southern Germany.

In course of time, however, the Latin language gradually changed.

In *Italy* Latin gradually changed into *Italian.*
In *France*   „     „     „     „  *French.*
In *Spain*   „     „     „     „  *Spanish.*
In *Portugal* „     „     „     „  *Portuguese.*

Thus Latin is the mother of Italian, French, Spanish, and Portuguese, and is a great help to us when we come to learn any of these. It is also of very great use in helping us to understand our own language, although Latin is not the mother of English.

You have learned in your English Grammar that there are five cases ;[1] but in Latin there are six, and the names of them are not quite the same. I will put them in two columns for you to compare them.

| English Cases. | Latin Cases. |
| --- | --- |
| 1. Nom-i-na-tive | 1. Nom-i-na-tive |
| 2. Voc-a-tive | 2. Voc-a-tive |
| 3. Objec-tive | 3. Ac-cu-sa-tive |

[1] The book referred to is *A Primary English Grammar*, by Theophilus Hall.

| English Cases. | Latin Cases. |
|---|---|
| 4. Poss-ess-ive | 4. Gen-i-tive |
| 5. Da-tive. | 5. Da-tive |
| | 6. Ab-la-tive. |

You have learned, too, in your English Grammar that a *Noun* is *declined* by putting it through all the five cases, both in the singular and in the plural.

Let us *decline* the word *Child* as we have done it in our English Grammar.

| Singular Number. | | Plural Number. | |
|---|---|---|---|
| *Nom.* | Child | *Nom.* | Children |
| *Voc.* | O Child | *Voc.* | O Children |
| *Obj.* | Child | *Obj* | Children |
| *Poss.* | Child's | *Poss.* | Children's |
| *Dat.* | Child | *Dat.* | Children. |

So too we decline a *Noun* in Latin by putting it through all the *six* cases, both singular and plural.

I will decline the Latin word *Mensa* (a table) for you : look at it well, but you need not learn it off by heart yet.

| Singular Number. | | Plural Number. | |
|---|---|---|---|
| *Nom.* | Mensa | *Nom.* | Mensæ |
| *Voc.* | Mensa | *Voc.* | Mensæ |
| *Acc.* | Mensam | *Acc.* | Mensas |
| *Gen.* | Mensæ | *Gen.* | Mensarum |
| *Dat.* | Mensæ | *Dat.* | Mensis |
| *Abl.* | Mensa | *Abl.* | Mensis. |

There are a great many nouns in Latin, but they are not all declined like Mensa. Indeed, there are five different ways in which nouns are declined, and these are called the *five declensions.* Every noun belongs to one of these five declensions, and I shall presently tell you how we know to which one any given noun belongs.

It will take us several weeks to learn these five declensions, so we must set to work slowly, and learn each one thoroughly as we come to it.  We will begin with the

## FIRST OR "A" DECLENSION,

so called because the STEM ends in *a*.  The nouns belonging to this declension are nearly all feminine, end in *a*, and are done like Mensa, the one above.  You will learn it most easily by committing to memory the case-endings, as under :

|       | Sing. | Plural. |      | Sing. | Plural. |
|-------|-------|---------|------|-------|---------|
| *Nom.* | ă     | æ       | *Gen.* | æ     | arum    |
| *Voc.* | ă     | æ       | *Dat.* | æ     | is      |
| *Acc.* | am    | as      | *Abl.* | ā     | is      |

Now I will give you a Latin vocabulary (that is, a list of words), with the English opposite.

## FIRST VOCABULARY.

*All these words are Feminine Gender.*

| | | | |
|---|---|---|---|
| Ăqua, | *water* | Lūna, | *the moon* |
| Āra, | *an altar* | Pæna, | *a punishment* |
| Aura, | *a breeze* | Porta, | *a gate* |
| Barba, | *a beard* | Rēgīna, | *a queen* |
| Cŏrōna, | *a crown* | Ira, | *anger* |
| Culpa, | *a fault* | Lingua, | *a tongue* |
| Fābŭla, | *a tale* | Stella, | *a star* |
| Fossa, | *a ditch* | Silva, | *a wood* |
| Hasta, | *a spear* | Via, | *a way* |
| Insula, | *an island* | Vita, | *life* |

(1) The above vocabulary must be learned by heart.

(2) Each Latin word must be declined (without the English).

(3) Each Latin word must be declined with the English as under:

| Singular. | | | Plural. | | |
|---|---|---|---|---|---|
| *N.* | Lună, | *the moon* | *N.* | Lunæ, | *the moons* |
| *V.* | Lună, | *O moon* | *V.* | Lunæ, | *O moons* |
| *Acc.* | Lunam, | *the moon* | *Acc.* | Lunās, | *the moons* |
| *G.* | Lunæ, | *of the moon* | *G.* | Lunārum, | *of the moons* |
| *D.* | Lunæ, | *to the moon* | *D.* | Lunis, | *to the moons* |
| *Ab.* | Lunā, | *by the moon* | *Ab.* | Lunis, | *by the moons* |

## QUESTIONS.

1. What is the Latin for " of the moons ? " What case is it ?

2. What is the sign of the Genitive case ? the Dative ? the Ablative ?

3. What different meanings may be given to the following words :—*Lunis, Fossa, Silvæ, Stellas ?*

4. Write down the list of English words given in Vocab. I, then close your book and write the Latin words opposite them.

5. Give any English words you know connected with Aqua, Corona, etc.

The Genitive case, then, is known by the sign "*of.*"

The Dative case by the sign "*to*" or "*for.*"

The Ablative case by the signs "*by,*" "*with,*" "*from,*" "*in,*" "*on.*"

*odel showing how Exercise* I *is to be done.*

| | | |
|---|---|---|
| *Of the water* | *Gen-sing.* | Aquæ |
| *With tongues* | *Abl.-plur.* | Linguis |

## Exercise I.

**A**

| | | |
|---|---|---|
| An altar | In the wood | The breeze |
| Of the beard | With faults | To the altars |
| To the gate | By life | For the queens |
| Of the island | To the altar | With a spear |
| In anger | For a queen | The stars (*acc.*) |
| The altar | From the woods | With spears |
| Of the beards | A gate (*acc.*) | |

**B**

| | | |
|---|---|---|
| The moons | The tale | O queen |
| From the island | By the beards | With anger |
| A tale | Of the islands | Of the altars |
| By the beard | For the queen | The ditches (*acc.*) |
| To the gates | Of the altar | Of a spear |
| Of the moons | The tale (*acc.*) | By the way |
| With a crown | In the water | |

## Exercise II.

**A**

| | | |
|---|---|---|
| Aquæ | Hastæ | Linguæ |
| Auræ | Silvis | Aris |
| Fossam | Insularum | Fabulis |
| Silvā | Arā | Stellis |
| Insulæ | Culpas | Portam |
| Aquarum | Pæna | Iras |
| Barbam | Silvarum | |

**B**

| | | |
|---|---|---|
| Fossas | Via | Culpam |
| Lunæ | Auram | Lunæ |
| Viam | Reginæ | Barbis |
| Aram | Irā | Vitas |
| Regina | Fabulam | Auras |
| Hastam | Vias | Portæ |
| Lunas | Aras | |

## THE SECOND OR "O" DECLENSION.

We have three lists of case-endings to learn this time
(1) for nouns ending in *us*, (2) in *er*, (3) in *um*.

Those ending in *us* and *er* are Masculine gender.

Those ending in *um* are Neuter gender.

### CASE ENDINGS, SECOND DECLENSION.

| | S. | P. | S. | P. | S. | P. |
|------|----|------|----|------|----|------|
| *Nom.* | us | i | er | i | um | a |
| *Voc.* | ĕ | i | er | i | um | a |
| *Acc.* | um | ōs | um | ōs | um | a |
| *Gen.* | ī | orum | i | orum | i | orum |
| *Dat.* | o | is | o | is | o | is |
| *Abl.* | o | is | o | is | o | is |

| | | | |
|------|------------|-------------|-----------|
| *Nom.* | Dŏmĭnŭs | Măgistĕr | Bellum |
| *Voc.* | Dŏmĭnĕ | Magister | Bellum |
| *Acc.* | Dominum | Magistrum | Bellum |
| *Gen.* | Domini | Magistrī | Bellī |
| *Dat.* | Dominō | Magistrō | Bellō |
| *Abl.* | Dominō | Magistrō | Bellō |

| | | | |
|------|------------|-------------|-----------|
| *Nom.* | Dominī | Magistrī | Bellă |
| *Voc.* | Dominī | Magistrī | Bellă |
| *Acc.* | Dominōs | Magistrōs | Bellă |
| *Gen.* | Dominōrum | Magistrōrum | Bellōrum |
| *Dat.* | Dominīs | Magistrīs | Bellīs |
| *Abl.* | Dominīs | Magistrīs | Bellīs |

## SECOND VOCABULARY.

*All these words are Masculine Gender.*

| | | | |
|-----------|-----------|---------|-----------|
| Agnus, | *a lamb* | Equus, | *a horse* |
| Ănĭmus, | *spirit* | Hortus, | *a garden* |
| Annus, | *a year* | Murus, | *a wall* |
| Campus, | *a plain* | Nātus, | *a son* |
| Dĭgĭtus, | *a finger* | Nummus, | *money* |

| Nŭmĕrus, | *a number* | Rivus, | *a stream* |
| Ŏcŭlus, | *an eye* | Servus, | *a slave* |
| Pŏpŭlus, | *the people* | Somnus, | *sleep* |
| Porcus, | *a hog* | Taurus, | *a bull* |
| Rāmus, | *a bough* | Ventus, | *the wind* |

| Ăger, | *a field* | Căper, | *a he-goat* |
| Ăper, | *a wild boar* | Cŏlŭber, | *an adder* |
| Arbĭter, | *an umpire* | Culter, | *a knife* |
| Auster, | *the south wind* | Lĭber, | *a book* |
| Cancer, | *a crab* | Minister, | *a servant* |

### Neuter.

| Antrum, | *a cave* | Ferrum, | *iron* |
| Argentum, | *silver* | Fŏlium, | *a leaf* |
| Bellum, | *war* | Ōvum, | *an egg* |
| Collum, | *a neck* | Sĕpulcrum, | *a tomb* |
| Dōnum, | *a gift* | Verbum, | *a word* |

The word *Puer*, a boy, does not go quite like Magister. I will now decline *Puer*, and do you try and find the difference.

| | Sing. | Plural. | | Sing. | Plural. |
|---|---|---|---|---|---|
| *Nom.* | Puer | Pueri | *Gen.* | Pueri | Puerorum |
| *Voc.* | Puer | Pueri | *Dat.* | Puero | Pueris |
| *Acc.* | Puerum | Pueros | *Abl.* | Puero | Pueris |

A few words only are done like Puer, the chief of which are

| Gener, | *a son-in-law* | Lĭber, *Bacchus* (only in sing.) |
| Socer, | *a father-in-law* | Liberi, *children* (only in plur.) |

### EXERCISE III.

| **A** Of the lamb | Of the walls | Hogs |
| For the year | To the son | To the slaves |
| With spirit | With money | With a stream |
| To the plain | Numbers | By a bull |

| | | |
|---|---|---|
| With a finger | Of the eyes | From the wind |
| For lambs | For the eyes | For a sleep |
| In the gardens | Hogs (*acc.*) | |

**B** Fields | By an adder | Crabs
| Fields (*acc.*) | With a knife | Of an adder |
| By a wild-boar | Books (*acc.*) | To the umpire |
| Of the south wind | With books | In a book |
| To the teacher | In fields | O teacher |
| Of teachers | For a knife | Knives (*acc.*) |
| Of crabs | By the servant | |

**C** Caves | An egg (*acc.*) | Of the boy
| With silver | To the tomb | Boys (*acc.*) |
| For war | In tombs | Of a son-in-law |
| On the neck | Of leaves | With children |
| Of the neck | With leaves | In an egg |
| Gifts (*acc.*) | For a word | With iron |
| By a word | By the neck | |

## EXERCISE IV.

| **A** | | |
|---|---|---|
| Agnis | Librorum | Ovo |
| Camporum | Tauri | Capri |
| Equi | Vento | Pueri |
| Equos | Arbitrum | Sepulcra |
| Muris | Collo | Verbo |
| Porcorum | Dona | Rivi |
| Rami | Ferrorum | |

| **B** | | |
|---|---|---|
| Bellorum | Somne | Ramos |
| Libri | Agno | Pueri |
| Aprum | Collis | Pueris |
| Servos | Ova | Libri |
| Equum | erborum | Liberi |
| Digitus | Oculis | Liberis |
| Muros | Ventum | |

# THE THIRD DECLENSION (CONSONANT AND "I" NOUNS).

This Declension will give us the most trouble, so we must proceed very carefully.

We said that in nouns belonging to the First Declension the Nominative case ended in *ă;* that in the Second Declension the Nominative ended either in *us, er,* or *um.*

But nouns of the Third Declension have so many different endings for the Nominative case that I cannot put them down in the table, so I shall put down *Various* instead.

The Vocative will always be like the Nominative.

There are two great classes of nouns belonging to this Declension :

(1) Nouns which have a syllable more in the Genitive than in the Nominative (called *Imparisyllable*).

(2) Nouns which have the same number of syllables in the Genitive as in the Nominative (called *Parisyllable*).

CASE-ENDINGS, THIRD DECLENSION.

| | Imparisyllable m. & f. | | Imparisyllable—Neuters. | |
|---|---|---|---|---|
| | Sing. | Plur. | Sing. | Plur. |
| *Nom.* | various | ēs | various | a |
| *Voc.* | ,, | ēs | ,, | a |
| *Acc.* | em | ēs | ,, | a |
| *Gen.* | is | um | is | um |
| *Dat.* | i | ibus | i | ibus |
| *Abl.* | ĕ | ibus | ĕ | ibus |

### EXAMPLES OF IMPARISYLLABLE NOUNS (MASC. AND FEM.).

| | Judex, *a judge.* | Leo, *a lion.* | Virgo, *a virgin.* | Lex, *a law.* |
|---|---|---|---|---|
| *Nom.* | Jūdex (*m*) | Lĕō (*m*) | Virgō (*f*) | Lex (*f*) |
| *Voc.* | ,, | ,, | ,, | ,, |
| *Acc.* | Jūdĭcem | Lĕōnem | Virgĭnem | Lēgem |
| *Gen.* | Jūdĭcĭs | Lĕōnĭs | Virgĭnĭs | Lēgĭs |
| *Dat.* | Jūdĭcī | Lĕōnī | Virgĭnī | Lēgī |
| *Abl.* | Jūdĭcĕ | Lĕōnĕ | Virgĭnĕ | Lēgĕ |
| | | | | |
| *Nom.* | Jūdĭcēs | Lĕōnēs | Virgĭnēs | Lēgēs |
| *Voc.* | ,, | ,, | ,, | ,, |
| *Acc.* | ,, | ,, | ,, | ,, |
| *Gen.* | Jūdĭcum | Lĕōnum | Virgĭnum | Lēgum |
| *Dat.* | Jūdĭcĭbŭs | Leonĭbŭs | Virgĭnĭbūs | Lēgĭbŭs |
| *Abl.* | ,, | ,, | ,, | ,, |

### EXAMPLES OF IMPARISYLLABLE NEUTER NOUNS.

| | Nomen, *a name.* | Opus, *a work.* | Caput, *the head.* | Corpus, *the body.* |
|---|---|---|---|---|
| *Nom.* | Nōmĕn | Ŏpŭs | Căpŭt | Corpŭs |
| *Voc.* | ,, | ,, | ,, | ,, |
| *Acc.* | ,, | ,, | ,, | ,, |
| *Gen.* | Nōmĭnĭs | Ŏpĕrĭs | Capĭtĭs | Corporĭs |
| *Dat.* | Nōmĭnī | Operī | Capitī | Corporī |
| *Abl.* | Nōmĭnĕ | Operĕ | Capĭtĕ | Corporĕ |
| | | | | |
| *Nom.* | Nōmĭnă | Ŏpĕră | Capĭtă | Corporă |
| *Voc.* | ,, | ,, | ,, | ,, |
| *Acc.* | ,, | ,, | ,, | ,, |
| *Gen.* | Nominum | Operum | Capitum | Corporum |
| *Dat.* | Nominĭbus | Operĭbus | Capitĭbus | Corporĭbus |
| *Abl.* | ,, | ,, | ,, | ,, |

NOTICE that in order to decline Judex, etc., you must know that the stem is Judic, and it is then easy to affix the case-endings you have learnt above. In the next vocabulary, therefore, I have given you the Nom. and Gen. cases. Cut off the *is* from the Gen. case, and it will tell you the stem.

Thus the stem of Lapis is Lapid.
    ,,     ,,    Sanguis is Sanguin
    ,      ,,    Lux is Luc

## THIRD VOCABULARY.

### Masculine.

| Pēs, | Gen., | pĕdis, | *foot* |
|------|-------|--------|--------|
| Lăpis, | ,, | lapĭdis, | *stone* |
| Grex, | ,, | grĕgis, | *flock* |
| Rex, | ,, | rĕgis, | *king* |
| Sāl, | ,, | sălis, | *salt* |
| Sōl, | ,, | sōlis, | *sun* |
| Sangŭis, | ,, | sanguĭnis, | *blood* |
| Carbo, | ,, | carbōnis, | *coal* |
| Ămŏr, | ,, | amōris, | *love* |
| Cardo, | ,, | cardĭnis | *hinge* |

### Feminine.

| Crux, | Gen., | crŭcis, | *cross* |
|-------|-------|---------|---------|
| Lux, | ,, | lūcis, | *light* |
| Pax, | ,, | pācis, | *peace* |
| Vox, | ,, | vōcis | *voice* |
| Rādix, | ,, | radīcis, | *root* |
| Uxor, | ,, | uxōris, | *wife* |
| Mors, | ,, | mortis, | *death* |
| Laus, | ,, | laudis, | *praise* |
| Mens, | ,, | mentis, | *mind* |
| Ōrātio, | ,, | oratiōnis, | *speech* |

### Neuter.

| Flūmen, | Gen., | flumĭnis, | *river* |
|---------|-------|-----------|---------|
| Fulmen, | ,, | fulmĭnis, | *thunderbolt* |

### Neuter—*continued*.

| | | | |
|---|---|---|---|
| Grāmen, | Gen., | gramĭnis, | *grass* |
| Frīgus, | „ | frigŏris, | *cold* |
| Tempus, | „ | tempŏris, | *time* |
| Lūmen, | „ | lumĭnis, | *light* |
| Sēmen, | „ | semĭnis, | *seed* |
| Funus, | „ | funĕris, | *death* |
| Pondus, | „ | pondĕris, | *weight* |
| Scĕlus, | „ | scelĕris, | *crime* |

### Exercise V.

**A** With the foot
To the flocks
Of the king
With salt
In the sun
Of a stone
With blood

In love
Of a hinge
From the light
For the king
With voices
By the roots
Of kings

O death
To the cross
Of wives
In a speech
To the light
For praises

**B** With the feet
For the flock
To the kings
Of salt
From the sun
Of stones
Blood (*acc.*)

Hinges (*acc.*)
O peace
To the cross
From suns
Stones
Roots (*acc.*)
With roots

In death
For a wife
O king
Of love
In the flock
With stones

**A** In the river
Of a thunderbolt
Grasses
In a crime
With a name
Of names
To works

With heads
Heads
Heads (*acc.*)
Of death
For the cold
Thunderbolts
Seeds (*acc.*)

Crime (*acc.*)
A body
Bodies
With a weight
For crimes
Rivers

**B** Solem
Laudis
Mente
Orationes
Tempore
Pacum
Pacem

Mortibus
Semina
Sanguinis
Regibus
Fulminum
Gramini
Lapide

Pedibus
Voces
Vox
Radices
Uxori
Lucem

### PARISYLLABLE NOUNS.

These nouns generally end in *es*, *is*, *e*, and a few in *er*.

Those ending in *es* are fem. gender, those in *e* neuter.

| | Nubes, *a cloud.* | Navis, *a ship.* | Mare, *the sea.* | Pater, *a father.* |
|---|---|---|---|---|
| *Nom.* | Nūbēs (f.) | Nāvĭs (f.) | Mărĕ (n.) | Pătĕr (m.) |
| *Voc.* | ,, | ,, | ,, | ,, |
| *Acc.* | Nubem | Navem | ,, | Patrem |
| *Gen.* | Nūbĭs | Navĭs | Maris | Patris |
| *Dat.* | Nūbī | Navī | Marī | Patri |
| *Abl.* | Nūbĕ | Navĕ | Marī | Patre |

| | | | | |
|---|---|---|---|---|
| *Nom.* | Nūbēs | Naves | Maria | Patrēs |
| *Voc.* | ,, | ,, | ,, | ,, |
| *Acc.* | ,, | ,, | ,, | ,, |
| *Gen.* | Nub*ium* | Nav*ium* | Mar*ium* | Patr*um* |
| *Dat* | Nubĭbus | Navĭbus | Maribus | Patrĭbus |
| *Abl.* | ,, | ,, | ,, | ,, |

**Notice** that the Imparisyllable nouns make the Genitive plural in **um**, whilst the Parisyllable ones make it in **ium.**

This is not always so, but it is so in all the words in your vocabulary.

### THIRD VOCABULARY—*continued.*

| Feminine. | | Masculine. | |
|---|---|---|---|
| Aedēs, | *temple* | Collĭs, | *hill* |
| Cædēs, | *slaughter* | Crīnis, | *hair* |

| Feminine. | | Masculine. | |
|---|---|---|---|
| Clādēs, | *defeat* | Ensis, | *sword* |
| Fēlēs, | *cat* | Ignis, | *fire* |
| Prōlēs, | *offspring* | Pānis, | *loaf* |
| Rūpēs, | *rock* | Feminine. | |
| Sēdēs, | *seat* | Ăvis, | *bird* |
| Strāgēs, | *destruction* | Auris, | *ear* |
| Vallēs, | *valley* | Ŏvis, | *sheep* |
| Vulpēs, | *fox* | Rătis, | *raft* |

## EXERCISE VI.

**A** Of slaughter

In defeat

For the cat

With fire

In a seat

O rocks

Of the valleys

On seats

By foxes

To the hills

In the hair

With a sword

With swords

For a loaf

From cats

Birds (*acc.*)

Bird (*acc.*)

O sheep (*pl.*)

On rafts

For offspring

**B** To slaughter

Of defeat

By the cat

In fires

For a seat

To the rocks

In the valleys

Seats

O foxes

Of the hills

In the fire

With swords

Of the ears

A loaf (*acc.*)

By the cat

For the bird

In the temple

On the raft

In the valley

To a seat

## THIRD VOCABULARY—*continued.*
### Neuter.

| Mărĕ, | *sea* | Mŏnīle, | *necklace* |
|---|---|---|---|
| Cŭbīle, | *bed* | Rēte, | *net* |
| Insigne, | *ensign* | | |

*Note.*—Păter, *father ;* Māter, *mother ;* Frāter, *brother ;* Senex, *old man ;* Jŭvĕnis, *a youth ;* Vatēs, *a prophet ;* and Cănis, *a dog,* ought, according to our rule, to make the Genitive plural in *ium ;* but they are *irregular,* and make it in *um.*

## *THE FOURTH DECLENSION ("U" NOUNS).*

Masculine and Feminine Substantives in this Declension end in *ŭs;* Neuters in *ū.*

The case-endings are as under :

|       | Sing. | Plur. |
|-------|-------|-------|
| *Nom.* | ŭs | ūs |
| *Voc.* | ŭs | ūs |
| *Acc.* | um | ūs |
| *Gen.* | ūs | ŭum |
| *Dat.* | ŭī | ibus |
| *Abl.* | ū | ibus |

### EXAMPLES.

| | Gradus (*m*), *step.* | Manus (*f*), *hand.* | Genu (*n*), *knee.* |
|-------|-------|-------|-------|
| *Nom.* | Grădŭs | Mănus | Genū |
| *Voc.* | „ | „ | „ |
| *Acc.* | Gradum | Manum | „ |
| *Gen.* | Gradūs | Manūs | Genūs |
| *Dat.* | Graduī | Manŭī | Genū |
| *Abl.* | Gradū | Manū | Genū |

| | | | |
|-------|-------|-------|-------|
| *Nom.* | Gradūs | Manūs | Gĕnŭă |
| *Voc.* | „ | „ | „ |
| *Acc.* | „ | „ | „ |
| *Gen.* | Gradŭum | Manŭum | Genŭum |
| *Dat.* | Gradibus | Manibus | Genĭbus |
| *Abl.* | „ | „ | „ |

## FOURTH VOCABULARY.

| Masculine. | | Feminine. | |
|-------|-------|-------|-------|
| Aestŭs, | *tide* | Ănus, | *old woman* |
| Căsŭs, | *accident* | Mănus, | *hand* |
| Currus, | *chariot* | Portĭcus, | *colonnade* |

| Masculine. | | Feminine. | |
|---|---|---|---|
| Exercĭtus, | *army* | Quercus, | *oak* |
| Flātus, | *blast* | Sŏcrus, | *mother-in-law* |
| Fluctus, | *wave* | Nŭrus, | *daughter-in-law* |
| Sensus, | *feeling* | Fīcus, | *fig* |
| Tactus, | *touch* | | Neuter. |
| Tractus, | *extent* | Cornū, | *horn* |
| Vultus, | *countenance* | Gĕnū, | *knee* |
| | | Gĕlū, | *frost* |

### Exercise VII.

| | | |
|---|---|---|
| With an accident | The countenance | In the oak |
| To the chariot | With the hand | Of chariots |
| In the army | With hands | With a touch |
| With feelings | The horns | Of the hand |
| To the touch | On the knees | To the waves |
| Of an old woman | In the blast | The tides (*acc.*) |
| For a fig | Of the countenance | |

---

## THE FIFTH DECLENSION ("E" NOUNS).

There are very few Nouns of this Declension, and they are of the *Feminine* gender.

The case-endings are:

| | Sing. | | Plur. |
|---|---|---|---|
| *Nom.* | ēs | *Nom.* | ēs |
| *Voc.* | ēs | *Voc.* | ēs |
| *Acc.* | em | *Acc.* | ēs |
| *Gen.* | ēī | *Gen.* | ērum |
| *Dat.* | ēī | *Dat.* | ēbus |
| *Abl.* | ē | *Abl.* | ēbus |

Res, *a thing*, and Dies, *day*, are the only nouns which are fully declined. Most of the others have only the Nominative, Vocative, and Accusative plural, and some have no plural at all.

### EXAMPLES.

| | Dies, day. | | | Res, thing. | |
|---|---|---|---|---|---|
| | Sing. | Plur. | | Sing. | Plur. |
| *Nom.* | Dĭēs | Dĭēs | *Nom.* | Rēs | Rēs |
| *Voc.* | Diēs | Dies | *Voc.* | Res | Res |
| *Acc.* | Diem | Dies | *Acc.* | Rem | Res |
| *Gen.* | Diēī | Diērum | *Gen.* | Rĕī | Rērum |
| *Dat.* | Diēī | Diēbus | *Dat.* | Rĕī | Rēbus |
| *Abl.* | Diē | Diēbus | *Abl.* | Rē | Rēbus |

---

## FIFTH VOCABULARY.

| Ăcies, | *edge* | Prōgĕnies, | *offspring* |
|---|---|---|---|
| Făcies, | *face* | Răbies, | *madness* |
| Glăcies, | *ice* | Scăbies, | *roughness* |
| Paupĕries, | *poverty* | Spĕcies, | *appearance* |
| Fĭdes, | *faith* | Spēs, | *hope* |

### EXERCISE VIII.

| | | |
|---|---|---|
| Faces | In affairs | Of hope |
| Hopes (*acc.*) | Of affairs | Of an appearance |
| On the face | For the day | For offspring |
| In poverty | O poverty | By an edge |
| Of the day | By days | By hope |
| Of the days | | |

Notice particularly the Genitive cases of all the Five Declensions.

|              | 1    | 2    | 3          | 4    | 5    |
| ------------ | ---- | ---- | ---------- | ---- | ---- |
| *Gen. sing.* | ae   | i    | is         | ūs   | ei   |
| *Gen. plur.* | ārum | ōrum | um or ium  | uum  | ērum |

---

## ADJECTIVES.

An Adjective must agree with the noun to which it belongs, in Gender, Number, and Case.

Thus an Adjective must have three Genders, so that it may agree with a Masculine noun, a Feminine noun, or a Neuter noun.

(1) Adjectives with *three endings* in *us, a, um,* or *er, a, um.*

The case-endings are as under, and you will notice that the Masculine column goes like Dominus, the Feminine column like Mensa, and the Neuter column like Bellum.

| Singular. | M. | F. | N. | Plural. | M. | F. | N. |
| --------- | -- | -- | -- | ------- | -- | -- | -- |
| *Nom.*    | us | a  | um | *Nom.*  | i  | æ  | a  |
| *Voc.*    | e  | a  | um | *Voc.*  | i  | æ  | a  |
| *Acc.*    | um | am | um | *Acc.*  | os | as | a  |
| *Gen.*    | i  | æ  | i  | *Gen.*  | orum | arum | orum |
| *Dat.*    | o  | æ  | o  | *Dat.*  | is | is | is |
| *Abl.*    | o  | ā  | o  | *Abl.*  | is | is | is |

### EXAMPLES.

#### Sing.

| *Nom.* | Bŏnŭs  | Bŏnă   | Bŏnum |
| ------ | ------ | ------ | ----- |
| *Voc.* | Bŏně   | Bŏnă   | Bonum |
| *Acc.* | Bonum  | Bonam  | Bonum |
| *Gen.* | Bonī   | Bonæ   | Bonī  |
| *Dat.* | Bono   | Bonæ   | Bono  |
| *Abl.* | Bono   | Bonā   | Bono  |

### Plur.

| *Nom.* | Bŏnĭ | Bŏnæ | Bŏnă |
|---|---|---|---|
| *Voc.* | ,, | ,, | ,, |
| *Acc.* | Bonos | Bonas | Bona |
| *Gen.* | Bonorum | Bonarum | Bonorum |
| *Dat.* | Bonis | Bonis | Bonis |
| *Abl.* | ,, | , | ,, |

### Sing.

| *Nom.* | Tĕnĕr | Tĕnĕră | Tĕnĕrum |
|---|---|---|---|
| *Voc.* | ,, | ,, | ,, |
| *Acc.* | Tenerum | am | um |
| *Gen.* | Teneri | æ | i |
| *Dat.* | Tenero | æ | o |
| *Abl.* | Tenero | ā | o |

### Plur.

| *Nom.* | Tĕnĕrī | æ | ă |
|---|---|---|---|
| *Voc.* | ,, | ,, | ,, |
| *Acc.* | Teneros | as | a |
| *Gen.* | Tenerorum | arum | orum |
| *Dat.* | Teneris | is | is |
| *Abl.* | ,, | ,, | ,, |

### Sing.

| *Nom.* | Nigĕr | Nigră | Nigrum |
|---|---|---|---|
| *Voc.* | ,, | ,, | ,, |
| *Acc.* | Nigrum | am | um |
| *Gen.* | Nigri | æ | i |
| *Dat.* | Nigro | æ | o |
| *Abl.* | Nigro | ā | o |

**Plur.**

| Nom. | Nigri | æ | ă |
|------|-------|-----|------|
| Voc. | ,, | æ | a |
| Acc. | Nigros | as | a |
| Gen. | Nigrorum | arum | orum |
| Dat. | Nigris | is | is |
| Abl. | ,, | ,, | ,, |

## SIXTH VOCABULARY.

### Like BONUS, *good.*

| Albus, | *white* | Magnus, | *great* |
|--------|---------|---------|---------|
| Altus, | *lofty* | Mălus, | *bad* |
| Arduus, | *steep* | Nŏvus, | *new* |
| Cārus, | *dear* | Parvus, | *small* |
| Dūrus, | *hard* | Rectus, | *straight* |
| Lātus, | *broad* | | |

### Like TENER, *tender.*

| Asper, | *rough* | Mĭser, | *wretched* |
|--------|---------|--------|------------|
| Lăcer, | *torn* | Prosper, | *lucky* |
| Lĭber, | *free* | Frūgĭfer, | *fruitful* |

### Like NIGER, *black.*

| Æger, | *sick* | Pulcher, | *handsome* |
|-------|--------|----------|------------|
| Noster, | *our* | Vester, | *your* |

## EXERCISE IX.

**A** Of a great altar

Of great altars

In a broad ditch

With a free tongue

New gates

With wretched horses

In a fruitful garden

Straight boughs (*acc.*)

Of a torn book

In a free island

**B**

| Lucky slaves | With a small leaf |
| Handsome girls | In a steep cave |
| For a sick servant | For hard eggs |
| By our Queen | With beautiful streams |
| Broad plains | In a rough wood |

(2) Other Adjectives follow the third declension, as you will see from Tristis, *sad ;* Melior, *better.*

|  | Singular. | | | Plural. | | |
|---|---|---|---|---|---|---|
|  | M. | F. | N. | M. | F. | N. |
| *Nom.* | Tristĭs | — | ĕ | Tristēs | — | ĭă |
| *Voc.* | Tristis | — | e | Tristes | — | ia |
| *Acc.* | Tristem | — | e | Tristes | — | ia |
| *Gen.* | Tristĭs | — | — | Tristĭum | — | — |
| *Dat.* | Tristĭ | — | — | Tristibus | — | — |
| *Abl.* | Tristi | — | — | Tristibus | — | — |

|  | M. | F. | N. | M. | F. | N. |
|---|---|---|---|---|---|---|
| *Nom.* | Melior | — | us | Meliorēs | — | ă |
| *Voc.* | Melior | — | us | Meliores | — | a |
| *Acc.* | Meliorem | — | us | Meliores | — | a |
| *Gen.* | Melioris | — | — | Meliorum | — | — |
| *Dat.* | Meliori | — | — | Melioribus | — | — |
| *Abl.* | Meliorĕ or ĭ | — | — | Melioribus | — | — |

## SEVENTH VOCABULARY.

### Like TRISTIS, *sad.*

| Brĕvis, | *short* | Hŭmĭlis, | *low* |
| Dulcis, | *sweet* | Sĭmĭlis, | *like* |
| Făcĭlis, | *easy* | Stĕrĭlis, | *barren* |
| Fortis, | *brave* | Utĭlis, | *useful* |
| Grăvis, | *heavy* | Nŏbilis, | *noble* |

D

### Like MELIOR, *better.*

| | | | |
|---|---|---|---|
| Altior, | *higher* | Gratior, | *more pleasing* |
| Fortior, | *stronger* | Dulcior, | *sweeter* |
| Clarior, | *brighter* | Utilior, | *more useful* |

### EXERCISE X.

**A**

| | |
|---|---|
| A brave king | To a short hill |
| With sweet love | On heavy rafts |
| Of a noble wife | Stronger foxes |
| With short grass | With heavy destruction |
| In a brighter speech | For a brave boy |

---

## *VERBS.*

You have learnt in your English Grammar that Verbs have Voices, Moods, Tenses, etc., but all I want to do now is to teach you the Six Tenses of the Indicative Mood, Active Voice.

There are four Regular Conjugations.

(*Note.*—Nouns are declined; Verbs are conjugated.)

We tell to which Conjugation a verb belongs by the ending of the *Present-stem.*

| 1st Conj. | A verbs | as, ămā-rĕ, | *to love* |
|---|---|---|---|
| 2nd „ | E „ | as, mŏnē-rĕ, | *to advise* |
| 3rd „ Cons. „ | as, rĕg-ĕrĕ, | *to rule* |
| U „ | as, indū-ĕrĕ, | *to put on* |
| 4th „ | I „ | as, audī-rĕ, | *to hear* |

The Six tenses of the Indicative Mood are:

| | |
|---|---|
| 1. Present Tense | 4. Perfect Tense |
| 2. Future Simple | 5. Future Perfect |
| 3. Imperfect | 6. Pluperfect |

## AMO, I LOVE.

### PRESENT TENSE.

| | | |
|---|---|---|
| 1. | Ăm-ō, | *I love*, (or) *I am loving* |
| 2. | Ăm-ās, | *Thou lovest*, (or) *Thou art loving* |
| 3. | Ăm-ăt, | *He loves*, (or) *He is loving* |
| 1. | Am-āmus, | *We love*, (or) *We are loving* |
| 2. | Am-ātis, | *Ye love*, (or) *Ye are loving* |
| 3. | Am-ant, | *They love*, (or) *They are loving* |

### FUTURE SIMPLE.

| | | | |
|---|---|---|---|
| 1. | Ămā-bō, | *I shall* | |
| 2. | Amā-bĭs, | *Thou wilt* | |
| 3. | Amā-bĭt, | *He will* | *love* |
| 1. | Amā-bĭmus, | *We shall* | |
| 2. | Amā-bĭtis, | *You will* | |
| 3. | Amā-bunt, | *They will* | |

### IMPERFECT.

| | | | |
|---|---|---|---|
| 1. | Ămā-bam, | *I was* | |
| 2. | Ama-bas, | *Thou wast* | |
| 3. | Ama-bat, | *He was* | *loving* |
| 1. | Amā-bāmus, | *We were* | |
| 2. | Amābātis, | *You were* | |
| 3. | Ama-bant, | *They were* | |

### PERFECT.

| | | | |
|---|---|---|---|
| 1. | Ămāv-ĭ, | *I have* | |
| 2. | Amāv-istĭ, | *Thou hast* | |
| 3. | Amāvĭt, | *He has* | *loved* |
| 1. | Amāv-ĭmus, | *We have* | |
| 2. | Amav-istis, | *You have* | |
| 3. | Amāv-ērunt, | *They have* | |

[FUTURE PERFECT.

| 1. | Ămāv-ĕrō, | *I shall* | |
|----|-----------|-----------|---|
| 2. | Amav-eris, | *Thou wilt* | |
| 3. | Amav-erit, | *He will* | *have loved* |
| 1. | Amav-erimus | *We shall* | |
| 2. | Amav-eritis | *You will* | |
| 3. | Amav-erint, | *They will* | |

PLUPERFECT.

| 1. | Ămāv-ĕram, | *I had* | |
|----|-----------|---------|---|
| 2. | Amav-eras, | *Thou hadst* | |
| 3. | Amav-erat, | *He had* | *loved* |
| 1. | Amav-erāmus, | *We had* | |
| 2. | Amav-erātis, | *You had* | |
| 3. | Amav-erant, | *They had* | |

*Notice.*—The *personal endings* Sing.-, *s, t.* Plur. *mus, tis, nt.*

The Imperfect is the *bam* tense, and the sign, *was.*

The Perfect always ends in *i*, and the sign is, *have.*

The Future Perfect always ends in *ero*, and the sign is, *shall have.*

The Pluperfect always ends in *eram*, and the sign is *had.*

When we give the Principal Parts of a Latin verb, we give the Present indicative, Perfect indicative, Supine and Present infinitive.   Thus the principal parts of Amo are :

| Ămō | Ămāvī | Āmātum | Ămārĕ | *to love* |
|-----|-------|--------|-------|-----------|
| Mŏnĕō | Mŏnŭ-ī | Mŏnĭtu-m | Mŏnē-rĕ | *to advise* |
| Rĕgō | Rex-ī | Rect-um | Rĕg-ĕrĕ | *to rule* |
| Audĭō | Audī-vī | Audĭt-um | Audīrĕ | *to hear* |

I will now put the Indicative Mood of these four Verbs in a tabular form for you.

## INDICATIVE MOOD OF THE FOUR CONJUGATIONS.

| | | | Singular. | | | Plural. | | |
|---|---|---|---|---|---|---|---|---|
| | | | **1** | **2** | **3** | **1** | **2** | **3** |
| **Pres.** · | Verb itself: *do; am* · | Am- | o | ās | ăt | āmŭs | ātĭs | ant |
| | | Mŏn- | eo | ēs | ĕt | ēmŭs | ētĭs | ent |
| | | Rĕg- | o | ĭs | ĭt | ĭmŭs | ĭtis | unt |
| | | Aud- | ĭŏ | ĭs | ĭt | īmŭs | ītis | ĭunt |
| **Fut.** · **Simp.** | *Shall; will* | Āmā-<br>Mone-<br>Reg-<br>Audi- | bŏ<br><br>am | bĭs<br><br>ēs | bĭt<br><br>ĕt | bĭmŭs<br><br>ēmŭs | bĭtis<br><br>ētis | bunt<br><br>ent |
| **Imperf.** | *Was* · · | Āmā-<br>Mone-<br>Reg-e<br>Audie | bam | bas | bat | bamus | batis | bant |
| **Perf.** | *Have* · · | Āmāv-<br>Monu-<br>Rex-<br>Audiv- | ī | isti | it | ĭmus | istis | ērunt |
| **Fut.** · **Perf.** | *Shall have* · | Āmāv-<br>Monu-<br>Rex-<br>Audiv- | ĕro | ĕris | ĕrit | ĕrimus | eritis | erint |
| **Plup.** | *Had* · · | Āmāv-<br>Monu-<br>Rex-<br>Audiv- | eram | eras | erat | eramus | eratis | erant |

Notice that the first three tenses are formed from the Present Stem, and that the last three tenses are from the Perfect Stem.

I will now give you a Vocabulary of A verbs and E verbs. All the A verbs will go like Ămāre, and the E verbs like Monēre.

## EIGHTH VOCABULARY.

### A VERBS.

Stem.

| | Stem. | | | | |
|---|---|---|---|---|---|
| Praise, | (Lauda-) | Laudo | Laudāv-i | Laudā-tum | Laudā-re |
| Plough, | (Ara-) | Ăro | Ărāv-i | Arā-tum | Arā-re |
| Strive, | (Certa-) | Certo | Certav-i | Certā-tum | Certā-re |
| Shout, | (Clama-) | Clāmo | Clamāv-i | Clamā-tum | Clamā-re |
| Swim, | (Nata-) | Năto | Natav-i | Natā-tum | Natā-re |
| Carry, | (Porta-) | Porto | Portav-i | Portā-tum | Portā-re |
| Sing, | (Canta-) | Canto | Cantav-i | Cantā-tum | Cantā-re |
| Call, | (Voca-) | Vŏco | Vocāv-i | Vocā-tum | Vocā-re |

### E VERBS, OR VERBS WHOSE STEM ENDS IN E.

Stem.

| | Stem. | | | | |
|---|---|---|---|---|---|
| Fear, | (Tĭme-) | Tĭmĕō | Tĭmu-ī | | Timē-re |
| Have, | (Hăbe-) | Hăbeō | Habu-ī | Habi-tum | Habē-re |
| Frighten, | (Tĕrre-) | Tĕrrĕō | Terru-i | Terri-tum | Terrē-re |
| Hold, | (Tĕne-) | Tĕnĕō | Tĕnŭ-ī | Tentum | Tenē-re |
| Teach, | (Doce-) | Dŏcĕō | Dŏcŭ-ī | Doc-tum | Dŏcē-rĕ |
| Laugh, | (Ride-) | Rĭdĕō | Rīs-ī | Ris-um | Ridē-re |

MODEL SHOWING HOW EXERCISE XI. IS TO BE DONE.

| Aramus | 1 pers. | plur. | present | We plough |
|---|---|---|---|---|
| Natabis | 2 pers. | sing. | fut. simp. | Thou wilt swim |

### EXERCISE XI.

| A Laudat | Portabis | Certaverit |
|---|---|---|
| Portamus | Risit | Laudavit |
| Vocatis | Clamaverat | Clamabam |
| Docet | Laudabit | Habemus |
| Tenuistis | Aras | Timebatis |
| Laudabat | Certabant | Natabunt |
| Natant | Terruerat | |

**B** Vocas
Natabam
Tenes
Laudavisti
Portabunt
Vocabat
Portavero

Docebant
Cantaverat
Portabant
Vocabis
Cantatis
Timebo
Canto

Terrui
Vocavit
Arabant
Ridemus
Cantabo
Timet

## EXERCISE XII.

**A** I will praise
We were swimming
I am ploughing
We teach
He was singing
You shout

They had striven
Ye will frighten
I have called
You are shouting
They laugh
Thou fearest

**B** He was ploughing
I am holding
They swim
Ye laugh
We will sing
I hold

I was carrying
They will laugh
You have taught
He will call
They strive
We sing

## NINTH VOCABULARY.

### VERBS WHOSE STEMS END IN A CONSONANT.

| | Stem. | | | | |
|---|---|---|---|---|---|
| Touch | (tang-) | tangō | tĕtĭg-ĭ | tactum | tang-ĕrĕ |
| Write, | (scrib-) | scrībo | scrips-ī | scriptum | scrīb-ēre |
| Conquer, | (vinc-) | vinco | vic-ī | vīc-tum | vinc-ĕre |
| Sell, | (vend-) | vendo | vendĭd-ī | vendĭtum | vend-ĕre |
| Cut, | (cæd-) | cædo | cecĭd-i | cæsum | cæd-ĕre |
| Lead, | (duc-) | dūcō | dux-i | ductum | dūc-ĕre |

## Verbs whose Stems end in I.

Stems.

| Punish, | (puni-) | pūnio | punĭv-i | punītum | punī-re |
| Come, | (veni-) | vĕnĭō | vēn-ī | ventum | veni-re |
| Fortify, | (muni-) | mūnĭo | munīv-i | munītum | munī-re |
| Sleep, | (dormi-) | dormĭo | dormīv-i | dormitum | dormī-re |
| Feel, | (senti-) | sentĭō | sens-i | sensum | sentī-re |
| Open, | (aperi) | aperĭo | ăpĕrŭ-i | apertum | aperi-re |

### Exercise XIII.

A  
| Tangit | Tetigit | Sentient |
| Ducit | Vendes | Vendunt |
| Scripserit | Aperuit | Duxerit |
| Vincam | Scripsit | Vendebant |
| Venis | Duxerat | Cæditis |
| Vincis | Vicerunt | Sentient |
| Duxit | Cecidisti | |

B  
| Tangebat | Dormiverunt | Scribet |
| Vincetis | Scripsi | Duxeram |
| Munitis | Sentiet | Cædunt |
| Duxeras | Ducebatis | Vēnit |
| Sentit | Vendidisti | Vĕnit |
| Vinces | Punit | Aperis |
| Tangunt | Scribit | |

### Exercise XIV.

A  
| They touch | We conquer | You will lead |
| I have punished | He sells | They sell |
| He had slept | You will have cut | I came |
| They have felt | I was conquering | You will write |

B  
| Ye open | He is sleeping | He comes |
| They fortify | They will sleep | He is coming |
| He has led | I had sold | He came |
| We were writing | They have opened | He had written |

# THE VERB "ESSE,"—*To Be.*

## INDICATIVE MOOD.

| PRES. TENSE - | 1 Sum | I am |
|---|---|---|
| | 2 ĕs | Thou art |
| | 3 est | He is |
| | 1 sŭmus | We are |
| | 2 estĭs | Ye are |
| | 3 sunt | They are |
| FUT.-SIMPLE - | 1 ĕro | I shall be |
| | 2 eris | Thou wilt be |
| | 3 erit | He will be |
| | 1 erĭmus | We shall be |
| | 2 erĭtis | Ye will be |
| | 3 erunt | They will be |
| IMPERFECT - | 1 ĕram | I was |
| | 2 eras | Thou wast |
| | 3 erat | He was |
| | 1 erămus | We were |
| | 2 eratis | Ye were |
| | 3 erant | They were |
| PERFECT - | 1 fŭi | I have been |
| | 2 fuistī | Thou hast been |
| | 3 fuit | He has been |
| | 1 fuĭmus | We have been |
| | 2 fuistis | You have been |
| | 3 Fuĕrunt *or* fuēre | They have been |
| FUT.-PERFECT | 1 fŭĕro | I shall have been |
| | 2 fueris | Thou wilt have been |
| | 3 fuerit | He will have been |
| | 1 fŭerĭmus | We shall have been |
| | 2 fŭerĭtis | Ye will have been |
| | 3 fuerint | They will have been |

## INDICATIVE MOOD—*continued*.

| PLUPERFECT - | 1 fŭĕram | I had been |
|---|---|---|
| | 2 fueras | Thou hadst been |
| | 3 fuerat | He had been |
| | 1 fuerāmus | We had been |
| | 2 fueratis | Ye had been |
| | 3 fuerant | They had been |

## CONJUNCTIVE MOOD.

| PRESENT - | 1 Sim | I may be |
|---|---|---|
| | 2 sis | Thou mayst be |
| | 3 sit | He may be |
| | 1 sĭmus | We may be |
| | 2 sitīs | Ye may be |
| | 3 sint | They may be |
| IMPERFECT - | 1 essem | I might be |
| | 2 esses | Thou mightst be |
| | 3 esset | He might be |
| | 1 essēmus | We might be |
| | 2 essētis | Ye might be |
| | 3 essent | They might be |
| PERFECT . . | 1 fŭĕrim | I may have been |
| | 2 fueris | Thou mayst have been |
| | 3 fuerit | He may have been |
| | 1 fŭerĭmus | We may have been |
| | 2 fŭerĭtis | Ye may have been |
| | 3 fuerint | They may have been |
| PLUPERFECT - | 1 fŭissem | I might have been |
| | 2 fuisses | Thou mightst have been |
| | 3 fuisset | He might have been |
| | 1 fuissēmus | We might have been |
| | 2 fuissētis | Ye might have been |
| | 3 fuissent | They might have been |

## IMPERATIVE MOOD.

| PRESENT · · | 1 | |
|---|---|---|
| | 2 ĕs | Be thou |
| | 3 | |
| | 1 | |
| | 2 estĕ | Be ye |
| | 3 | |
| FUT.-SIMP. · | 1 | |
| | 2 esto | Thou must be |
| | 3 esto | He must be |
| | 1 | |
| | 2 estōtĕ | Ye must be |
| | 3 suntŏ | They must be |

## VERB INFINITE.

| | | | |
|---|---|---|---|
| INFINITIVE MOOD | Present and Imperfect } | esse | To be |
| | Perfect and Pluperfect } | fuisse | To have been |
| | Future | fŏre *or* fŭtŭrus esse, | To be about to be |
| PARTICIPLE | Future | fŭtŭrus | About to be |

THE END.

# The following Approved School Books are now greatly reduced in price.

**Turrell's French Phraseology.** 1,000 Oral Exercises in French Phraseology, Idioms, and Synonyms. By H. S. TURRELL, M.A. Seventh Edition ... price 2s.

**Turrell's French Reader ;—Leçons Françaises,** De Littérature et de Morale, en Prose et en Vers ; ou, Nouveau Recueil de Morceaux, extraits des Meilleurs Auteurs. By H. S. TURRELL, M.A. Third Edition, enlarged .. ... ... ... .. ... price 2s.

**White's First Greek Lessons.** A Course of Study, arranged by CHARLES WHITE, M.A., Cambridge. Each Lesson is preceded by a Vocabulary. Copious Index Verborum. Eighth Edition ... ... ... price 1s.

**First Principles of General Knowledge.** In Question and Answer. By Mrs. PAULL. Edited by Mr. DAVENPORT. Fourth Edition ... ... price 1s. 6d.

---

**Relfe's Numerical Report Books, for Boys' Schools.** Containing in each page a Weekly Report of every variety of Scholastic Exercise, on a plan affording either to Parent or Tutor a permanent Record of the application of the Pupil ... ... ... ... ... price 6d.

**Relfe's Numerical Report Books, for Young Ladies' Schools.** On the Plan of the above, but adapted to the Scholastic pursuits of Young Ladies ... price 6d.

\*\*\* Specimen pages forwarded to the Heads of Schools.

---

**Edwards' School Boys' Introduction to Book-keeping by Double Entry.** An entirely New Work on Double Entry, by JOHN EDWARDS ... ... price 1s.

THE KEY, consists of the complete set of books, contains the whole of the transactions properly arranged, with Balance Sheet showing the result of Six Months trading price 3s.

RULED BOOKS in which to re-enter and work out the set are prepared, manufactured from a superior paper.
Price 2s. the complete set.

---

LONDON : RELFE, BROTHERS, ALDERSGATE.

www.ingramcontent.com/pod-product-compliance
Lightning Source LLC
Chambersburg PA
CBHW021452090426
42739CB00009B/1728